T0208248

Let's Talk about
Hair

Also by Lynn Gauthier

One Book, One Bird, One Verse

Let's Talk about
Hair
The Truth beyond the Looking Glass

LYNN GAUTHIER

iUniverse, Inc.
Bloomington

LET'S TALK ABOUT HAIR
The Truth beyond the Looking Glass

iUniverse books may be ordered through booksellers or by contacting:

iUniverse
1663 Liberty Drive
Bloomington, IN 47403
www.iuniverse.com
1-800-Authors (1-800-288-4677)

Because of the dynamic nature of the Internet, any web addresses or links contained in this book may have changed since publication and may no longer be valid. The views expressed in this work are solely those of the author and do not necessarily reflect the views of the publisher, and the publisher hereby disclaims any responsibility for them.

Any people depicted in stock imagery provided by Thinkstock are models, and such images are being used for illustrative purposes only.
Certain stock imagery © Thinkstock.

ISBN: 978-1-4759-9014-0 (sc)
ISBN: 978-1-4759-9015-7 (ebk)

Library of Congress Control Number: 2013908263

Printed in the United States of America

iUniverse rev. date: 05/03/2013

Contents

In memory of my father

Preface

God's grace isn't found in a mirror, at least not in any mirror that I've ever looked into. Perfection isn't found in a mirror either, but that's where I continued to seek it.

In late March 2009, at age fifty-three, I recognized patterns of behavior in myself that paralleled my father's behavior. In 1975, at age fifty-four, my dad "divorced" his family and married the bathroom mirror. We didn't notice his preoccupation with his appearance right away, but it slowly robbed him and our family of the close relationship we could have had with him otherwise. He became the center stage of our disdain.

In March 2009, after weeks of morning journal entries, I was appalled by the monotony of my writing, which reflected my behaviors, namely my struggle with getting my bangs perfect and the frequent trips to the mirror that wasted countless hours. Typically, my journal since 1987 has been and remains my devotion time—a time to talk to God while I listen for answers, my pen scribbling away, page after page. I have stacks of journals that I don't know what to do with, as if I've been waiting for a book revelation to shake me and scream, "Write about this!"

So one day, after writing a lengthy prayer to God with specific reference to my hair struggles, I experienced an overwhelming release. The joy of the Lord overcame me in the form of laughter that not only affected me but brought delight to my husband and our three daughters. Something spoken at lunch that afternoon ignited an outburst of laughter that I could not control. My children were excited to watch me double over with laughter. They had no idea what was happening to me, but I knew that the Holy Spirit was doing a mighty healing in me and through me. The days that followed my breakthrough were not totally carefree, but new levels of self-acceptance crept in. After that, when I looked into the mirror, I approved. I always knew that I had God's approval, but the striving for perfection slowly dropped off. For the first time in years I was content with my appearance.

One year later, the idea for a book came to me. I recalled hair stories from my youth, hair episodes with my daughters, and conversations with my close friends about our hair. Hair had been a central theme all my life, and I knew I had to write about it.

My journey through hair stories—and non-hair stories—is my testament to faith, healing, love, and at last self-acceptance. There is life and truth beyond the looking glass.

"The Lord does not look at the things man looks at. Man looks at the outward appearance, but the Lord looks at the heart" (1 Samuel 16:7 NIV).

Acknowledgments

To my three beautiful daughters, Taisha, Tangela, and Tyrayna, who share one bathroom, one mirror, and at least one hair story a day, and to my wonderful husband, John, who manages to put up with the four ladies he lives with. Through all the laughter and the tears, you have brought joy into my life more than you know.

Chapter 1

Journaling

Three months of monotonous excerpts read from my daily journal brought me to May 2009 and my decision to let go and place my hair stress and my vanity into the hands of God.

3/12/09

I can't believe that I'm in the middle of another hair dilemma and that it always involves my bangs. I trimmed my bangs two days ago; a few snips here and there made a huge difference. But I look like a little Dutch boy. It happens repeatedly.

3/17/09

I can't figure out the whole bangs thing. I was trying to part them on the left side and that did not look right, so now the part is back on the right side. I'm not sure about that either.

4/1/09

Yesterday I liked my hair. I kept long bangs and pulled the sides back while leaving the back hanging loose. Face-framing bangs look good on me I think. They are youthful and sassy.

4/27/09

I am faced with mounds of laundry today, and my house is a mess, calling for my attention. But all I can do is look in the mirror and fuss over my hair. I want it to look chic. If I cut my bangs again, I will be discouraged and regret yet another attempt to find perfection in the mirror.

5/1/09

Having good hair this week has helped my state of mind. When my hair performs well, I don't give it much thought. I just want to be content.

5/5/09

I bought a fake ponytail, cut it up, and had fun attaching it to my hair.

5/6/09

I have been consumed by my hair all morning, looking in the mirror and trying to get it right. I almost decided to have it all chopped off.

5/7/09

I started the day off all right; I drove the kids to school, went to my school committee meeting, and came home. I did a little exercise and worked an hour at my art desk, but my mind was on my hair. This vanity enslaves me. It is seducing me to pick up the scissors again. Its force is so bizarre that I can hardly concentrate on the things at hand. It reminds me that I am my father's daughter, a victim of my heredity.

Tonight I lost the battle. I succumbed and took up my scissors again. I spent hours of wasted time in front of the mirror and ended the evening drunk on my own foolish vanity. This has been a week spent in pitiful self-absorption. I have been lassoed by the enemy of my life: my vanity. While I spoke of it the other day, it continues to plague me. Alas, I went to the hairdresser yesterday because I had an idea for a new hairstyle. When I arrived at the salon and showed the stylist a photo of the style I liked, she talked me out of it. She told me that I would hate it.

"I can give you an all-over trim to clean it up a little, and you should grow out your side layers. I'll blend your bangs so they won't look so choppy. I'd encourage you to leave haircutting to the professionals." With that said, she prepared me for the cut.

When I got back home, no one thought I had been to the hairdresser. There was no evidence of change. I pray about many things in my life, but I never thought that hair would make it on my prayer list. But, Lord, I am asking you to help me in my agonizing search for the right hairstyle. There's no end to this vain search for perfection. I let go of any preconceived ideas about how I want to look. Guide me to the right hairstyle and help me to be content with my overall appearance. The bathroom has become my playing ground. I am fearfully aware of how closely my behaviors resemble my father's. His years of struggling with his vanity led to mental illness. I don't want to spend my days like this anymore. Help! I have lost my joy. I have been on this wicked treadmill long enough, and today I'm getting off. Today is Mother's Day, and I am going to celebrate my new freedom. I want to see the God who made me, who loves me, who will pick me up and hold me when I fall down. Thank you for the victory that is mine, in Jesus's name, amen.

Mother's Day 2009 was a turning point for me in this journey to recovery. I speak of my hair dilemma as my addiction. It cannot be compared to drug addiction or alcoholism but it controls me in much the same way. My mind obsesses over my appearance, my hair in particular. My hair has rarely been a showstopper; my crowning glory has never gotten much glory.

Three years ago, while I was vacationing in Florida, a hairstylist made a keen observation.

"You have a couple of thinning spots at the back of your head you know."

My hair was already fine in texture, so I didn't need a couple of thinning spots to add to my troubles. Once in a while I'd come close to having a good hair day, but it usually fell short of my ideal; what I'd see was never what I wanted to see. I continually failed to get it perfect.

When did all this fuss about my hair begin?

Chapter 2

Mirror, Mirror on the Wall

Mirrors are everywhere; the bathroom, the bedroom, the car, restrooms, hotel rooms, dressing rooms, restaurants, just everywhere. As long as there are mirrors there will be deception. The mirror has been my biggest motivator to initiate change. It has sent me flying to the nearest drugstore for the miracle creams that promise to erase wrinkles and transform my hair from frumpy to fabulous. I've been in front of age-defying mirrors that mysteriously soften the look of my aging complexion, and I've stood in front of ruthless reflectors that magnify every crease, spot, and gray hair. It is all in the lighting. Florescent lighting is the worst offender. Sunlight, depending on the angle, runs a close second.

An entire vacation can be ruined if the mirror in the bathroom is unkind. I have spent days of vacation time distressed because I hated how unflattering I looked in the mirror. Does my skin look that bad? Is my hair that drab looking? I would ponder these questions all week long.

My father, Cono, was a handsome man and remained so well into his sixties. He was taut and fit, and he took great pride in his appearance. He loved to compare himself to men his age that had not fared as well. He adored his youthful physique. During his years of wellness, he was confident, gentle, and easy mannered. Good words flowed from his lips—words of hope inspired from evenings spent poring over the writings of great authors such as Dale Carnegie and Norman Vincent Peale. He listened to hours of tape recordings from successful men in sales and would try to imitate their winning attitudes. My father craved success.

In 1967, he took a job at Prudential Life Insurance working as an agent/broker. His dreams of financial freedom were always the next big sale away. The insurance job consumed him. He rehearsed his sales pitches in front of anyone who would listen. I was convinced that the bathroom mirror was his favored audience.

One day, in the middle of one of his bathroom performances, he spotted an ingrown hair on the left corner of his chin. This discovery marked the beginning of his downward spiral into mental illness. The ingrown hair led him to obsessive behaviors—not right away, but day by day as he wasted moments, hours, and then years laboring over that hair. He squeezed it, picked at it, stretched the skin around it, rubbed it, and then rubbed it more until it looked like the sore of a leper.

Am I my heavenly Father's daughter, made in the image and likeness of His glorious Son, Jesus Christ, or am I my earthly father's daughter, born with fine, flyaway hair, a potted complexion, strangled by my vanity and drawn to the mirror that ruined my father's life?

My father's frame of reference narrowed to the frame of the medicine cabinet mirror in our bathroom. His reflection became his world view. He could not move beyond this short range. His brain suffocated from the monotony of his own stale thoughts. He became irrational and self-absorbed. When he spoke, his thoughts were random and disconnected from reality

Life moved past my father as our family celebrated marriages, the birth of grandchildren, and the usual milestones that mark one's life. He never even noticed. After retirement he became a full-time prisoner to the bathroom mirror. The bathroom remained his solitary confinement for the last twenty years of his life. The ingrown hair left a scar that immobilized him.

On the morning of September 9, 2001, my father died from an infected gallbladder. He did not recognize the thief who stole away his years and robbed him of the vitality that could have been his. Vain habits took their toll over his lifetime and did their mischief so subtly that he was blinded to their destructiveness.

I am grateful to God for quickening my awareness. I, too, began the descent into that same world that kept my father in chains for years. It sounds ridiculous to think that a bathroom mirror could have that much power. But it became a magnet that attracted my vanity. I made a decision not to allow it to sabotage God's plan for my life. I thought of getting rid of all the mirrors in the house, but that would not have solved a thing. Mirrors have found and attracted me with fierce tenacity. Some days I could resist, but other days I was lured in to linger in front of a mirror and stand by while it hurled negatives at me and shattered my self-image.

It was scary for me to witness the repetition of my father's behaviors playing out in my life. In fact, it took years before it became apparent to me that I had inherited his vanity. Even as a child I was preoccupied with my hair and my overall appearance. I fussed over my skin and my hair. Even my nails had to be painted to match every outfit. It had to be right. No, it had to be perfect.

Chapter 3

Short Hair Nightmare
in Middle School

Growing up, my mother used to tell me that I looked like a little Indian girl with a head full of dark hair that stood straight up from the scalp. Looking back at old photographs from my childhood, my bangs went straight across the middle of my forehead. My mother liked bangs, very short bangs. I hated my short bangs. I vowed that if ever I were to have a daughter, I would never cut her bangs too short. Anyway, my mother had her way with my hair until I reached middle school. I liked long hair. It didn't matter what condition it was in as long as it was long.

I entered middle school in 1968. It was the Age of Aquarius, the Vietnam War, hippies, and love power. The school's dress code was transitioning from traditional skirts and dresses for girls to dress pants or pantsuits. Society was rapidly changing; it seemed okay to do things counter to the generations before us. We were a generation becoming freer, more open to personal expression, wherever that would lead us. I flowed with the tides of change. It was the perfect time to grow out my bangs and acquire the look of the day in teenage America: long straight hair parted in the middle. Most of my girlfriends in middle school came from Greek backgrounds. They were born with gorgeous, shiny, dark brown hair. Their locks were luscious, thick, and I craved what they had. It was painful to watch my girlfriends walk down the school corridors with their hair bouncing and swinging side to side while mine lay limp and flat.

In class the friend sitting behind me often reminded me how many split ends I had. I became the split-end detective, looking for every damaged strand that I could find and attacking with a hint of twisted pleasure.

My bangs grew out and finally dipped below my eyebrows. I styled them with a sweep across my forehead just grazing my right eye.

"Take those bangs out of your eyes." "How can you see with those bangs in your eyes?" "I'm going to cut those bangs for you if you don't do something about them." "Wear them pushed back. I can't stand looking at you!" The remarks and threats from my mother continued throughout my middle school years.

Hairspray helped. I could painstakingly arrange my bangs just the way I wanted and then aerosol them into a stiff mold. It was my idea of perfect. It evidently pained my mother so much that she decided to take action. She made an appointment for me with a real hairdresser. I didn't go to hair salons in my early youth. I guess it was easier for my mother to take care of the regular maintenance of trimming bangs and touching up the ends. Wetting my bangs down first was her biggest mistake. She would wet them flat against my forehead and snip across my brow. When they dried, the bangs would rise up at least an inch or more, making me look like a square picture frame. I'd spend the next few weeks crinkling up my forehead to make my bangs appear longer. I hated my short bangs.

I'm not sure if she talked me into getting a short haircut or if she just demanded it, but nonetheless, there I sat in the merciless seat of a male stylist who chopped away my hair to please my mother—certainly not me. He probably tried to convince me that the style he created was the latest chic hairdo and was recently seen on some runway in Paris. I looked awful. My bangs were shorter than ever and so choppy that they barely dropped below the line of my forehead. My hair was gone, most of it. My mother was delighted to see my forehead once again. My heart was in my throat when we left the salon.

Upon reaching the parking lot, the tears ran down my cheeks and dampened my face with sadness the rest of the weekend. Maybe I could transfer to a new school, I hoped.

Monday arrived. I grew weak at the thought of all the glaring eyes that would chase me down the school corridors that morning. I felt ugly. My image was ruined, and I was about to have that confirmed by a jury of my peers.

I arrived to school later than usual that morning. On the car ride there, my father, who was brilliant at giving pep talks, tried to convince me that my entire world had not just collapsed.

"Your hair will grow back, honey," he assured me. I was not encouraged, just frightened.

I walked into my first period English class past my classmates and dashed to my seat in the center of the room. The silence was haunting. Every stare stabbed me, and I knew in my gut that everyone hated my new haircut. The English teacher went right on teaching, and no one said a word. I bent over my desk with my head in my hands and sobbed. This was the worst public embarrassment that I had ever experienced. I let my hair grow out and didn't visit a hairdresser again for the next five years.

Chapter 4

Tennille

In the summer of 1974, just before my sophomore year of college, I planned a camping trip to Lake George, New York, with my boyfriend and my two cousins. We bought a canvas tent, a Coleman lantern, a two-burner propane stove, and two sleeping bags. We borrowed a suitcase and filled it with old cooking utensils, an old coffeepot from my mother, and some scratched up pots and pans. Life on the camping trail was going to be an exciting, new adventure for all of us.

Managing our outdoor dining arrangements and meal planning was the least of my challenges. I was not concerned about thunderstorms or sleeping on the hard ground in the tent or even snakes and black bears. What troubled me was the management of my hair. Needing to wash it daily was a luxury I would have to forego at the camp. My bangs would twist and curl and my oily scalp would create more trouble than I would care to deal with on vacation. The concern over my hair was a weighty matter even then. When my hair looked good, I just plain felt good. I therefore spent the first two days of my vacation overthinking my hair.

By midweek the heat and humidity of early August were demonizing my hair strands. Every glance I could steal in a gift-shop or car window brought me that much closer to craving an extreme makeover.

There was a beauty shop along the main street of the bustling tourist town in Lake George, and by Thursday I was lured into the salon and rallied on by my three camping mates. It was ecstasy just to sit in the swivel parlor seat, lean back, and have someone pamper and fuss over me. This was my first visit back to a salon since ninth grade.

The Captain and Tennille was a popular husband and wife musical duo in the mid 1970s. Female vocalists often wore fashionable hairstyles that would set in motion a universal craze. Well, Tennille wore her hair angled around the frame of her face and the length stopped at the base of her shoulders. The ends curled under like an angled bob and there was vitality and bounce in every step that she took. My vacation hairstylist talked me into the Tennille cut.

An hour later, I walked out of the salon feeling like a movie star. My hair looked perfect. I had faith in hairdressers once again. This was the best hairstyle that I ever had, and everyone who saw it showered me with compliments.

"Your hairstyle is so pretty!"

"I love that hairstyle on you!"

I loved the attention that my hair was getting. For the first time in my life my hair was a showstopper.

When we got back from vacation, I learned how to master the blow-dryer so I could recreate this masterpiece repeatedly. My hair routine was effortless until the style began to grow out. I could not return to Lake George to find the same stylist, so I decided to try my neighborhood salon.

Chapter 5

Elaine

Image Makers was the name of the hair salon located four blocks from my house. The salon had six stations that lined the perimeter of the small space. There was a receptionist at the front desk as you walked in. She answered the phone and set up appointments. In the center of the room were six hair dryers set up back to back and a sloppy pile of assorted women's magazines sitting on a glass table off to the side. In every chair sat gray-haired ladies pinned up in tiny rollers and hairpins under heated dryer hoods. They all looked alike. It was a beauty parlor for old ladies from my eighteen-year-old perspective. The place reeked of permanent ammonia, and the floor was decorated with fluffy, white hair clippings.

After giving my name to the receptionist, she asked, "Will you be having a shampoo, cut, and blow-dry today?"

I hesitated and then said, "No, I think I'd like just a trim." I've learned that you never tell a stylist that you want your hair cut because it then gives them license to cut more than what you intended. Saying that you just want a trim is a safer bet.

I like to arrive at least fifteen minutes early to a salon so that I can look through styling magazines. The receptionist directed me to sit down and said someone would attend to me shortly. While I waited, I glanced through some of the styling books that sat on the table in front of me. After a few moments a blonde woman in her late twenties walked over to greet me. Her name was Elaine. She brought me over to her station and sat me down on the cushiony salon seat. I liked her immediately. She extinguished the cigarette that she was smoking in the ashtray on her cluttered counter. Strewn all over her workstation were hairclips, a blow-dryer, a curling iron, cups of bobby pins, rollers, combs and brushes, her opened purse, and a pack of Winston brand cigarettes near the filthy ashtray. I liked her haircut. Elaine's hair was shaved around her left ear and the style graduated down past her earlobe on the right side. It was a clever asymmetrical cut that framed her boyish features beautifully.

She went about busily cleaning up her station while asking me, "Did you see something you liked in the book?"

The truth was, I saw plenty of styles that I loved if my hair was thick and long, but I was resigned to keeping the same Tennille cut.

"Not really. I think I'll just settle for a trim," I said.

Elaine caught a glimpse of herself in the mirror, tousled her hair, and went to work on me.

Over the years, I have discovered the difference between an excellent beautician and one who is mediocre. It is all in how they perform the shampoo. The better stylist, if you can bear it, will attack your scalp with wincing pressure and massage every inch as if she were kneading bread dough. Elaine was a pro.

After the shampoo, she harshly towel dried my hair and ran her fingers through my scalp to find my natural part. I was thoroughly entertained while she worked on me. She would grab a few strands of hair, taut between her fingers, then clip with her scissors and repeat the process with the next few strands. She then pulled the hair forward to check if each side matched evenly. She worked quickly and precisely. Before I knew it, she was ready to blow-dry and style my hair. Blow-driers were the popular hair tools of the 1970s. She used the round brush and the blower to sculpt my hair into a roll around my face. My hair felt smooth. It was shiny and a bit shorter than my previous cut, but I loved it.

I was comfortable with Elaine, and I called her my hairdresser for nearly twenty years. I was not always a regular customer, but she could count on my walking into the salon at least three times a year. I would call spontaneously, and she would always fit me into her schedule. Best of all, she never scolded me for getting scissor-happy in between cuts. She worked with me through many styling phases. After I grew tired of the Tennille cut, I had her crop my hair short over my ears in the front and left the back to hang in a shoulder length bob. Next, I went through a phase of experimentation with permanents and asymmetrical cuts, long shags, and chin-length bobs

Elaine worked magic on my fine tresses and never pressured me into trying new hair products or sticking to bimonthly appointments. She heard me through the drama of my high school prom, my first marriage, my divorce, the escapades of my single years, and my second marriage.

On the morning of my wedding day to my second husband, John, Elaine opened the salon at 8:00 a.m. just for me. It was a glorious, early autumn morning; the neighborhood was still waking up. I strolled to my appointment with my heart light and my head reeling with anticipation for my great day of celebration that had finally arrived. When I walked into the salon, Elaine was aglow and eager to tailor my hair to fit the large brimmed white hat that I had purchased only one week before. When she was finished, Elaine made me feel beautiful and sent me off to be married.

After the wedding was over and the work of my new life had begun, I started to practice thrift. My budget could not bear the cost of regular haircuts and interval trims, so I returned to the practice of cutting my own hair. I loved to fool around with hair. I groomed my French poodle, trimmed my aunt's hair, and did my ex-mother-in-law's hair for years. People trusted me with the scissors even though I often failed at my own vain attempts with cutting my hair. I should have pursued a career in hair design.

Actually, I did enroll in a school of hairstyling in fall 1978, in the age of big permed hair, the jogging craze, and disco dancing. My training lasted all of three weeks.

Chapter 6

Three Weeks at Hairdressing School

By the summer of 1973, my hair had grown long and style-less. I wore my bangs long, just grazing my eyebrows. I was a recent high school graduate working full-time as a retail clerk in our downtown art store. My goal was to save enough money to fund the trip I had planned to Hawaii in mid-August just before starting college in the fall. My life was getting busier. My hair and how it looked was not my main focus, so the same style graced my head for nearly four years. My hair had grown long again and that left me content.

I had half hopes of becoming a social worker; whatever I thought that was at the age of seventeen. At thirteen, I wanted to become a fashion model like Millie the Model, my favorite comic book idol. When I turned fourteen, I knew that I wanted to travel, so I decided that I would become an airline stewardess. By the time I reached the age of fifteen, a career in journalism seemed the ideal vocation. I loved to write, particularly poetry. In those days, I was streaming off a poem a day. My boyfriend of four years was the lucky recipient of my fine work; enough to publish an entire collection of love poems I was sure. I never kept copies so there are no archives to search through. So journalism it was until the end of my junior year of high school. I thought of joining the Peace Corps or finding work in the capacity of helping people. Probably something I read in English class tugged at my heart and ignited a new direction, an illuminated path. Actually, when it was time to choose a college, my decision rested on one thing: my boyfriend.

I was afraid to go away to school, to leave my boyfriend, my stable routine life, my parents . . . my bedroom.

In September 1973, I decided to enroll at the College of Our Lady of the Elms. My decision came from all my fears rather than my desire to break free. The college was located ten minutes from my house, an easy commute. The fact that it was not a coed campus put my boyfriend at ease. My career choice of social work added a noble tag to my repertoire of small beginnings. It was the perfect plan and put a loose bandage over all my fears.

During this time I grew my hair long and loved it. I didn't have time to fuss over it during my college career. I was too busy working hard as full-time student. I maintained a high level of achievement while I continued to work part-time in the local art shop and spend time with my boyfriend.

By early fall of my sophomore year, I got engaged. Our plan was to be married by the end of the summer before the start of my junior year. My itinerary grew complicated with the added tasks of planning a wedding, apartment hunting, and then fixing up our new home. While my list of chores seemed endless, my hair, shaped in my then-new Tennille cut, was the one stable, comfortable thing in my life. It never lost its shape on the days of harsh weather. It was easy to care for and perfect for my entry into adulthood.

A shocking revelation rattled my heart and tormented my mind with doubt three weeks before the wedding. I was falling in love with the new intern at my place of employment. He was an irresistible, charismatic college grad being groomed to come into the family business. He arrived at the most inconvenient time in my life. My heart raced when he passed by me. The rumor in the workplace was that he was engaged to be married sometime in late fall. My wedding was planned and nearly underway, so I was safe and figured these stupid, hypnotic symptoms would quickly pass. So I got married at the end of August, and a few weeks later the intern called off his engagement. His change in plans had nothing to do with me but, it was about to complicate my future. I could not easily move forward in my new marriage while I continued to work with the man whom I was hopelessly attracted to. It became apparent very quickly that I had married the wrong man. I could no longer trust my emotions. My love for my husband cooled, and my heart escaped with the fantasy that carried me through long days and even longer nights of confusion and fear.

All was well with my hair; it continued to maintain its shape and was trouble-free. The image I saw in the mirror was far more attractive than the sin-stained condition of my heart, which was sinking deeper into desire and betrayal; a secret only God and I shared. I was not a religious woman, but I believed that God existed and He didn't take too kindly to impure affairs of the heart. I went to church enough in my youth to know the difference between heaven and hell, and I knew the seriousness of the betrayal I was toying with. In my Catholic upbringing, adultery was considered a major sin punishable by spending eternity in hell. I knew that I had to make a decision. I could follow my heart's lead, expose my desire, leave my marriage, and accept the consequences of spending eternity in hell, or I could deny my troubled emotions, stay married, and burn in despair the rest of my life. Eternity and the idea of hell were too far off into the future to worry about, so I decided to expose my desire and leave my marriage of four and a half months.

The romantic notion that my life could be fulfilled by a love that only then lived in my imagination was what motivated my decision to give up my marriage and chase the dream.

During the first month of my separation, the details of my life settled into neat compartments and a false contentment rested over me. My life was going to be perfect once the divorce was final and I could start a new relationship with the man who captured my heart.

The second month of my separation surprised me, however. I had left my first love, had to wait for my hoped-for love, and was introduced to a new love: his name was Jesus Christ. During my waiting period, a friend named Brian invited me to a prayer meeting at a friend's house. I got the directions, decided I had nothing to lose, and went to the meeting. That night changed my life. I learned about redemption and forgiveness and a love so profound, one found only in Jesus Christ. My sins were forgiven by a God so big that I yearned to learn more about his amazing love and grace. I bought a Bible and searched its pages to find all that I could about my new love.

Over the course of the next two months, I attended Bible classes, frequented prayer meetings, and clung tight to the truths

I was learning. Slowly, I felt the Holy Spirit urging me back to my marriage.

In the third month of my separation, I returned to my husband. Upon our reconciliation, I left my job and walked away from the life that could have been. In the months that followed, I picked up every book that I could on the subject of marriage success. I learned how to cook, to clean, and to pray. I learned to enjoy being a married woman but I failed to love my husband enough. The only constant, sure thing in my life was my hair and God.

I made my regular visits to Elaine to have my hair trimmed. The Tennille style was the perfect balm during this year of zigzagged emotions. Feeling good about my appearance was important to me and it affected the way I'd react to my present concerns. I had God in my life, but I had not grown enough spiritually to know whom my true balm was. At this stage of my life, my hair was a big source of my confidence and helped determine how the world perceived me.

What did I want to do with my life? This was a question that nagged me like an old, tired spouse. Wasn't I supposed to be happy now that I was cleansed from my sin and had chosen to follow the word of God? I had returned to my marriage, left the job that I loved, and was working painfully hard at trying to be the perfect wife. I was miserable. A new career could be the answer to fill the void that hung over most of my days. I did not want to return to college. I wanted to do something that I loved, so I enrolled as a part-time student in hairdressing school.

Most students were fresh out of high school and enrolled full-time. I felt awkwardly out of place. Despite my best efforts, my marriage was breaking up for the second time, so learning how to do finger waves and being taught the fundamentals of the proper manicure were not exactly filling my cracked plate. The timing of this new endeavor was all wrong. Three weeks of hairdressing school was all I could handle. So I withdrew from my enrollment and promptly took on the full-time work of piecing my life back together.

Chapter 7

Meeting John

In the winter of 1984, I changed jobs three times, my Oldsmobile needed major engine repair, and my new boyfriend died in a horrible car crash. I was twenty-eight years old, single, and desperate for my life to take a new direction. I was certain that God was testing my faith. During this time, attending church was not my top priority. I dabbled and doubted and didn't take God very seriously. I loved him and suspected that he was waiting patiently for me, but my one nagging desire was to meet the man who would become my life partner.

For four years following my divorce, I tried to enjoy my single life. I had fun meeting new people in my social circles, but the man of my dreams was elusive. I fell in love a few times, or so I thought, and then assumed that the new man of the moment would become my future husband. Then something would happen, sometimes something very subtle, and the relationship would end suddenly.

After the divorce, I grew tired of the Tennille cut. I experimented with several new styles, including ones that were severely short. I wasn't going to hide behind my hair anymore.

By late March, I was working as an instructor at a women's fitness club in my town. As a new hire, I began training to lead classes in the new form of exercise known as aerobics training, a heart-pumping, pulse-pounding workout. I spent weeks searching out music to fit my forty-five minute routine, and I attended training classes in the evening after my shift was over. I enjoyed the benefits of great exercise but hated the sales aspect of the job. I had to make daily calls to prospective members who had expressed an interest in buying a club membership. My salary was directly affected by the ratio of sales I made over the week, which was often only a few. My paycheck suffered along with the many muscles that ached throughout my body from the daily workouts. I hated the job. I could not understand why some women would put themselves through those rigorous routines just to lose a few pounds. A walking program suited me better, and I bet I could have sold more women on that idea.

Anyway, during this time, even my short hair was uninteresting to me and hard to maintain. It exposed more of my face and brought attention to my troubled post-adolescent skin. In fact, I did not like much about myself during those gloomy March days. I was unhappily single, restless, and unsure about my future.

One night after my late training session, I stopped at Dunkin' Donuts, bought two coffees, and headed to my best friend's house for a surprise visit. I had my workout clothes on and my hair was sweaty, but amongst good friends, who cared?

When I arrived at her door, my friend alerted me that she had male company.

"Hey, come in. John's here. I'll introduce you."

"Oh, no, I don't want to intrude, and besides I look a mess."

"Nonsense, you look fine." She led me to the table where her male guest sat, but her phone rang before she could introduce us.

Across the table was a young, rather nice-looking man whom I assumed was my friend's new love interest. We had spent nights talking about him while munching on pretzels and drinking coffee and going on and on about how crazy she was about him. I didn't really need to be introduced; I felt like I knew him. He was the man who had swept her off her feet and onto the dance floor only months ago.

However, he was much younger than I imagined him to be, and frankly I was disappointed. I pictured her with someone older, a sophisticated gray-haired, ruddy-cheeked man. John looked like a fresh-faced grad student, polished and far too clean-shaven. I apologized to him for my appearance and intrusion. He was friendly enough and certainly engaging as we exchanged small talk while my friend continued with her phone conversation. I stayed for a short time, finished my coffee, and then said my good-byes to the two of them. I couldn't wait to go home, wash my face, and go to bed. It had been a long day.

Well, something other than what I thought to be my worst hair day attracted John to me that night.

Two months later, after several attempts at tracking me down, once at my workplace and then at a dance club in town where I would meet friends, John asked me out. I flatly declined at first. It was ludicrous; the idea of going out with my best friend's new boyfriend! He assured me that they were just friends who went out occasionally, certainly nothing serious. I'm not sure that she had the same take on this casual relationship that he described. Anyway, I agreed to one meeting, strictly platonic, I told him. We made plans to meet at a nearby reservoir to go running. I was not a runner, so I figured he could run slowly while I walked fast.

He never showed up for our running date. I was partially relieved and a little disappointed because I was mildly intrigued with his interest in me. I enjoyed the attention, but I hated the mounting guilt. The man who had just stood me up was drawing me into the same charismatic hold that had overtaken my friend.

Later the next week I learned that John spent the night in the hospital recovering from an asthma attack. He had run in a road race the day before our date. The midday heat had fatigued him. It all became clear why he didn't call. We'd never exchanged phone numbers, so he had no way to contact me. I felt better after my friend relayed this news to me.

In the weeks to follow, the relationship between John and my friend paled, much to her chagrin. The more she chased him, the more evasive he became. I watched in the shadows, hoping that in time they would part ways and my nesting emotions could hatch. She had no knowledge of my mounting interest in John.

One evening in late May, my friend invited me out; just her and a few working friends for a girls' night out at the dance club we frequented. On the car ride to the club that night, she bent over and whispered in my ear, "I know I told you that I was going to stop calling John, but I couldn't help myself. I called and left a message on his answering machine. I told him that we were all going out tonight and hoped he would meet us." A surge of anxious thoughts wheeled in the pit of my stomach as I forced a smile and thought about how awkward the evening would be.

As soon as we entered the club, our feet began tapping and the beat of the band was already rushing through our veins. Who cared what the evening would bring? I just wanted to dance. I was ready to circle the dance floor and rock my hips in jubilant celebration, celebrating nothing in particular. We ordered our beverage and took our place at the rail overlooking the dance floor. Behind where we stood, men and women brushed by us to place their orders at the bar; it was the usual bustling of a Thursday-night crowd. As the evening hastened, every available nook was filled with bodies; no one ever sat down. Either you stood mingling with friends or you danced. Part of the excitement was the familiar faces, the regulars who manned their posts and stood in their same pews.

After about an hour of small talk over drinks, I looked toward the entrance, and there he was. He walked tall as he moved through the crowd. Time paused as he made his entrance. I caught his eye, and we stayed on each other with an electric force so great that I forgot my moral compass and the impact this would have on my best friend, who was standing by my side. The attraction between us mounted suddenly and neither one of us could dismiss it.

John joined our group, and we exchanged casual greetings. He went to the bar, ordered a beverage for himself, and returned, asking my friend to dance. I slipped into the ladies' room, fussed over my hair a bit, lingered at the mirror while wishing my hair was longer, and then took a deep breath before returning to my post.

They returned from the dance floor fifteen minutes later, and before I could speak, he took my hand and led me onto the dance floor. I made nothing of it and followed his lead. When we arrived on the floor, the band slowed to a soft, romantic beat from the hit song" Hello" by Lionel Richie. John drew me into his embrace, and we danced for what seemed like an hour. He held me close and sang me the song as if he had written it just for me. His dance moves were smooth and certain, and I followed his lead with precision. We were perfect together, and we both knew it. I was hooked, and there was no question that something very powerful had just happened; there was no backing down.

When the song finally ended, we returned to find my friend watching us. John approached my friend for the next dance. I looked away and prayed that my face was not reflecting my captured heart. When they returned, the band took a break, and we engaged in more small talk, as if nothing peculiar had just happened. Maybe she had not noticed his obvious attention toward me or maybe she was silently digesting the truth unraveling before all of us. Nonetheless, when the band started playing again, John foolishly asked me to dance again, and I carelessly accepted. It was not long into the next dance that my best friend figured out that her two favorite people, the two people whom she had revealed her secrets to and had pure respect for, were openly betraying her. She stormed onto the floor, flung my jacket at me, and abruptly left the building. I had just fallen in love with the man by my side and lost my best friend in the same moment.

God's grace is amazing. John and I were married two years later, and God restored my relationship to my dear friend. She eventually met a great guy, and they too got married several years later. Happy endings do exist, and my hair had nothing to do with the outcome of any of these matters of the heart. Thank God!

Chapter 8

On the Last Day of Vacation

On February 26, 1986, I smoked my last cigarette. I was getting married in the autumn of that year and decided that I'd start my new married life smoke-free. I made a plan to let go of tired, old habits. I wanted to breathe easier and enjoy the confidence that comes with acquiring a healthier lifestyle. I succeeded. I quit smoking and made a vow to myself that I would save the money I would have spent on cigarettes and transfer it to a vacation fund.

My new lifestyle included a walking program that led to more conversations with God. I started spending more time playing my piano and keeping my hands busy with my calligraphy pens, which led to journaling. And best of all, I planned to take a vacation every year.

When it came to vacations, it will come as no surprise that the overwhelming urge to have my hair restyled nagged at me until our final day of vacation. I'm not sure if it was the mirrors in the resort bathrooms or the luxury of having a few extra dollars to spend on an impulse purchase, but every vacation ended up at a salon on the last day.

In late July 1992, John and I planned a two-week camping vacation to Tennessee and coastal Virginia with his two sons. One week before our excursion, I decided to give myself a new hairstyle. I chopped the sides of my hair to frame my face and add some soft layers. Once I decided to snip, the adrenaline surge was so powerful that I couldn't stop. I cut until the sides lay limp and uneven. I convinced myself that I could work with it by creating a windswept look that would adapt to our carefree vacation days. Anyway, I needed an unfussy style that would withstand the wind, dirt, and sun of days without shampoo. It bothered me a little that my hair was not properly cut, but it was obvious to no one but me.

The humidity of the South was worse than I could have imagined. My hair was too short on the sides to gather up into a ponytail, and without hairspray the result was pockets of frizz multiplying daily. I did not stop obsessing about my hair even once. The only thing I wanted to do on this vacation was visit a hair salon. Thank God hair salons were plentiful in Virginia Beach! With money in my wallet and a hair salon on every corner, I wasted no time making a hair appointment.

The next day, I was seated in the salon asking the stylist to fix my mangled crop. She obliged and the end product was a short bob. But it was chin-length and drab. The style screeched boring and did nothing to flatter me.

The vacation ended. The boys returned home, and I returned to my faithful stylist, Elaine, whom I knew could repair the damage.

I arrived at the salon fifteen minutes early so I could flip through some fashion magazines to inspire me with some ideas on what to do with my hair.

"What do you have in mind?" Elaine inquired. So I told her my hair story and fully submitted to whatever suggestions she had to help me recover any remaining style and regain my self-esteem. I was almost convinced that my hair would look better cut severely short. I yearned for something new and borderline dramatic.

"You could go short, or I could give you an asymmetrical cut and leave your left side chin-length, cropping the right side shorter. I think it would look really good on you, and it would be something different." I loved the idea and trusted her to make me look terrific. She did. The new design was fabulous; I was thrilled! My hair dilemma was over with, at least for a little while.

This was to be my last short haircut. In the years that followed, I wore my hair either at shoulder length or an inch or two longer. Elaine left her position at Image Makers, so instead of finding a new stylist I started the compulsive habit of trimming my own hair again. But almost every vacation, I end up in a salon on the last day.

Chapter 9

Going Blonde

I bought my first box of hair dye when I was thirty-two. The random gray strands started showing up since my twenty-fifth birthday. I occasionally plucked them out, but I could not afford to thin out my already-thin hair. I even tried to embrace the new gray strands. I was almost compelled to grow old gracefully until I was waiting on a male stylist one evening in the art department where I worked as a retail clerk.

The man was a known specialist in his field of hair design and highly sought out by many of the professional women who worked in the area. He was a local celebrity of sorts. He walked into the art department that evening, and I was instantly intimidated, but oddly intrigued, by his prettiness. He arrived at the register carrying an assortment of fine sable paintbrushes and tubes of Windsor Newton oil paints. As I stood at the register ringing up his sale, I caught him staring at me with particular emphasis on my head.

"You should do something about those gray hairs. You're too young to have gray showing . . . at least not until you turn fifty." He stated it so matter-of-factly that I hurried out to buy myself a box of semi-permanent hair color.

I had no prior experience with hair dye. I had to trust my instinct and the directions that came with the box. Semi-permanent color seemed to be a safe way to experiment. The mistakes, if any, would fade away in three weeks.

After two years of regular maintenance using the temporary hair color, I advanced to permanent color. This new route opened up a wider palette of tint choices and gave me the option to experiment with lighter shades. My dark brown hair was aging me as my gray hairs were multiplying. The gray roots were peeking through faster than I could keep up. Over the years I had memorized and catalogued enough beauty tips to know that ash tones were a better match for my skin type than warm or golden tints, so I began my experimenting with medium ash-brown tints. I enjoyed the results of the lighter shades.

Every summer, after spending time under the sun, I would notice my hair lighten. My medium brown hair would soften to light brown and even dark blonde. My gray hairs were blending in better with the lighter shades, and gradually my hair lightened so naturally that hardly anyone, including myself, remembered that I was once a dark brunette.

I became a blonde. Blonde hair suited me and covered my ever-accumulating gray strands effortlessly. I was forty-something and soon to be the adoptive mother of my first daughter. I was old enough to be her grandmother, but I didn't want to look like an older mom, so I kept the grays hidden with light ash-blonde tints.

Chapter 10

Bad Hair Day

I knew before I left the house that during our visit to the hair salon someone was going to try selling me hair products that would revolutionize my twelve-year-old daughter Taisha's crown of glory.

I held the six-inch tube in my hand for a few moments, turned it around discreetly to check the price, which read thirty-five dollars, and returned it to the hand of the stylist.

"This looks like a great product, but I don't think I'll be making a purchase today." *Thirty-five dollars for a tube of miracle gel? You've got to be kidding!* I thought. Thirty-five dollars would buy a tank of gas in my car, or better yet, a shampoo and cut for myself on our next vacation. My daughter would have that tube used up in two weeks, and my monthly budget would be destroyed for the sake of taming my daughter's mane. I wish I'd taken the time to look at the ingredients contained in that tube of gel because I bet a two-dollar jar of petroleum jelly would produce the same results.

Anyway, after two hours of hair treatment, including shampoo, conditioning cream, cut, blow-dry, and finally straightening with the flat iron, my daughter walked out of the salon looking like a high-fashion Barbie doll. Her locks of curls and frizz were gone, replaced by long, straight, sleek black hair.

Taisha bounced out of the salon that afternoon flipping her head from side to side, sweeping her long bangs from her eyes and thanked me endlessly for allowing her to have a real makeover in a real salon. The salon she'd been used to was the toilet seat in our small bathroom featuring Mom as the chief stylist. I have to admit that she looked very attractive in her new look.

Hair issues had ensued from the start of September, when she entered seventh grade. A new morning routine with an early bus to catch translated into a time crunch that couldn't afford an extravagant thirty-five minutes to be lavished on hair details. I decided that a visit to a hair salon would be the answer to end her hair woes.

Later that afternoon as I was walking in the woods behind our house, enjoying the fresh, warm air that often lingers in early September, I glanced over at my daughter who was riding her bike. I cringed. Her hair had doubled in volume and her long sleek strands had disappeared under a mass of frizz. The new hairdo was unraveling before my eyes! By evening, the salon experience and the cool new hairdo were but a memory. The clock had struck midnight, and by morning Cinderella's hair problems had returned. No glass slipper, no fairy godmother, and no thirty-five-dollar miracle cream were at hand to whisk away her troubles.

My daughter was growing up. Hair struggles were only the beginning of the list of challenges that lay wait for all of us during adolescence. There were no instant remedies. Her childhood fairy tales were just that—fairy tales—and her dreams of looking like her favorite pop star were in vain. She missed the school bus twice because of too much time spent on her hair, but in time she would learn to manage her personal needs so that she was never late.

I stopped being her hairdresser. Some days were better than others, but as she learned to manage her own styling I learned to let go. Her time spent on her hair dwindled to a mere fifteen minutes instead of the agonizing thirty-five. I must confess that my choice not to purchase the thirty-five-dollar miracle cream was the best purchase I never made.

Chapter 11

Free Haircut in Montgomery

By the time I reached my fiftieth birthday, I was trimming my hair on a regular basis and rarely making hair appointments. I trimmed my bangs every few weeks, always careful not to cut too much.

I was happily married with two adopted daughters. My oldest daughter Taisha was thirteen and Tangela, the youngest, was six. I was enjoying my life as a wife and mother, and I spent my leisure time painting in watercolors or writing. I wore my hair shoulder-length and flipped at the ends with a side part and bangs. My style was casually simple and easy to manage most days.

One evening in October 2006, my family attended a fundraiser for my children's dance center. An auction was set up with many beautiful items arrayed along the back wall of the large community hall where the ball was held. We purchased ten dollars' worth of tickets. After looking over all the items, we selected our favorites and then proceeded to drop our tickets in the jars that were placed in front of each gift item. One of the items was a twenty-five-dollar gift certificate to a hair salon located in Montgomery, Massachusetts. The owner and operator of the salon was the mother of one of the dance students.

At the conclusion of the evening, the names were drawn, and we became the happy recipients of the hair certificate. Well, my girls were not nearly as excited as I was because they had their heart set on some of the other great prizes. I was not sure which one of us would get the haircut, but I looked forward to making the appointment.

A month passed since the night of the fundraiser, and Christmas was only a few weeks away. I never did get around to making that appointment. By this time the certificate was a forgotten piece of paper tucked in an envelope that sat in my underwear drawer until the day after Christmas; the day before my fifty-first birthday. Traditionally, the day after Christmas was my time to clean drawers, tidy up spaces, and sweep away the past year's tired outfits and worn out items. This day, however, was dedicated to packing the family up in preparation for our trip to Virginia on December 29.

As I was sorting through my clothing, making piles and deciding what to bring on vacation, I came across the gift certificate. *A birthday makeover*, I thought. What a treat it would be to have my hair professionally styled—and just in time for vacation. Impulsively, I called to make an appointment. There were no openings on the twenty-seventh, so I booked an appointment for the morning of the twenty-eighth.

Montgomery is a little town way up in the hills of Massachusetts, about an hour's ride from my home in Becket, a small town in the Southern Berkshires. I was looking forward to this little bit of self-indulgence. The gift certificate, intended for one of my daughters, selfishly became mine.

I didn't have a specific hairstyle in mind. I just wanted the stylist to even out my ends and maybe transform my bangs into the perfect frame for my eyes.

When I arrived at my destination, I parked my car in the driveway of a newly constructed home in the middle of nowhere. The door was open, so I walked in and saw a woman whom I immediately recognized from the dance center. We exchanged greetings and then shifted into the reason for my being there, my hair.

"I want to keep the length. I think a little layering here and there may plump up the volume and give it a healthier look. I also want to keep the bangs long," I said. She nodded in agreement and walked me over to the sink.

She was a tall, lean, and attractive woman maybe in her mid-thirties. She had two daughters who were both students of the dance center. The salon was located in the finished basement of her home. It had only one salon seat, a few waiting chairs, a sink, and a counter that housed hair products. It was a great set-up for an at-home business.

I let her wash my hair because I wanted the full pampering that the certificate offered. After the shampoo, she sat me in the salon seat. Next, she prepared her tools, one being a razor. The last time anyone used a razor on my hair was the male stylist who ruined my hair when I was a kid with my mother. I didn't dwell on it and trusted that she knew what she was doing. My confidence grew as I learned that she was the daughter of a beautician and had been around hair and hair products her entire life. So she placed the razor between her fingers and cut my fine strands, layer by layer. When I caught a glimpse of myself in the full mirror in front of me, I realized what a grave mistake I had made.

Two days before, while in the dressing room of a thrift shop where I was trying on some jeans, I was pleased with how good my hair looked. So why was I there in that chair being butchered with a razor? I hoped that when she finished it would somehow look great. Besides, I could always touch it up when I returned home as was my usual custom.

When she finished the razor cut, she took up her blow-dryer, whizzed it around my head, and plugged in her straightening iron. I tried keeping my eyes lowered to avoid seeing myself in the mirror. That awful "something is not right" feeling that you get when you know that you just made the worst decision of your life was making knots in my stomach. The flatiron was heated and ready. She straightened my bangs in three sections and then unplugged her iron and finger-styled the rest of my hair.

"Let me show you the back," she said and then picked up her hand-held mirror to give me a view of the back of my head. Choppy. All I could see was choppy, messy hair. I gulped, got out of my seat, forced a smile, gave her my certificate, and handed her a ten-dollar tip.

"Would you like to set up your next appointment in about six weeks?" she asked.

"Oh, I think I'd better wait and check my calendar. I have your card, so I'll call you."

As soon as the door of the salon closed behind me, I knew I would never return.

When I got in my car, I looked at myself in the rearview mirror and could not believe the ruin that framed my face. The hour drive home felt like three.

Once home, I headed straight for the bathroom before anyone in my house could see me. Unfortunately, my daughter Taisha came around the corner before I reached the bathroom. She checked me out with a puzzled look.

"So what did you have done? It kind of looks the same."

"Not much," I answered off-handedly and went straight into the bathroom. I threw my coat on the hamper and turned to face the mirror. I stared at myself for a moment and then got a little closer to the mirror. I could not make sense of the bangs. What did this woman do to my bangs? Not only were they brittle, they were brassy yellow and mismatched with the rest of my hair. They were not the same bangs I started out with before the hair appointment. On further scrutiny, they felt coarse like the texture of a scouring pad and smelled like ammonia or a chemical that is used in permanent coloring. I tried wetting them down, combing them, stretching them, and finally straightening them with my flat-iron. I couldn't soften them or make them look better, so I took out my scissors and cut them. Two inches of dried, dead hair fell into the bathroom sink. Even two inches didn't remedy the problem that faced me. I was left with very short, brittle bangs that would take at least four months to grow out. I wanted to hide. I couldn't stop looking at myself in the mirror hoping that a miracle solution would appear like a genie from a magic bottle.

Chapter 12

My Miracle

There are no magic solutions and genies that pop out of bottles to grant you three wishes. However, there are wigs, fake ponytails, and hair extensions. I have played with add-on bangs, braided hair bands, and clip-in hair extenders. They are all fun to experiment with until they increase daily maintenance and add too much fussiness to everyday routines.

Hair is a hot topic. I have two wonderful friends whom I can engage in lengthy conversations about their hair or my hair or the hair we wish we had. The hair that sits atop our heads is our crowning glory. Imagine, God has numbered all the hairs on our head and He knows about every strand that falls out. He is interested in how we look because He created us and is pleased with His handiwork. I don't believe that He wants us to allow our vanity to consume us. We are made in His image and likeness and it is the inner man whom He is more concerned about. God specifically states, "Your beauty should not come from outward adornment, such as braided hair and the wearing of gold jewelry and fine clothes. Instead, it should be that of your inner self, the unfading beauty of a gentle and quiet spirit, which is of great worth in God's sight" (1 Peter 3:3, 4 NIV).

Does it have to take a lifetime to reconcile one's appearance and become comfortable in the skin we were born with? As long as there are people who have silkier hair, smoother skin, and shapelier bodies than our own, we may struggle with an image that falls short of our measure. Our eyes are a great gift and yet they curse us when we seek perfection.

As the years passed, I've grown in maturity in the knowledge and understanding of God's Word. God loves me whether my hair is long, short, blonde, gray, or flyaway. The quality of my life is not determined by the kind of hair day that I am having, or for that matter the kind of hair day my kids are having. I have three daughters now, all with wavy, course hair, and every day at least one of them is having a hair crisis. My ten-year-old, Tangela, crumbles when her straightened bangs get a raindrop on them when she walks outside. My nine-year-old, Tyrayna, wears a blanket over her head when she gets out of bed, lest anyone should see her messy hair, and my eighteen-year-old, Taisha, complains constantly about her puffy hair that she just smeared with globs of hair gel. It's funny because it has caused me to look at my own fine tresses with gratitude that I don't have their hair woes.

What does hair have to do with God? I tell my children that everything has to do with God and hair is no exception. Hair is our covering. If we are fortunate enough to have it on our heads, it protects us, shields us from the elements, and keeps us warm. It can also give us much trouble and become the focus of our lives. Hair keeps growing as sure as night and day keep revolving. If we cut our hair too short, it will eventually grow back. It has a redeeming quality like the very nature of God.

I've arrived at an age that my children consider old. Fifty-something-plus sounds old to a fifth grader who looks in the mirror every day and only sees eternal youth. I want my children to enjoy the skin and hair they were born with. I want them to cease striving for the perfect hair or body that they were not born with. It has taken me a lifetime to learn these truths. I have made peace with my hair. The scissors are no longer my assault weapon and the mirror is no longer my enemy most days. I have not made a hair appointment in months, and I still prefer long hair to short.

I've learned to take all my concerns to God in prayer. He hears and sees it all and cares about every detail in my life. God has blessed me with the miracle of contentment.

"But Godliness with contentment is great gain"

(1 Timothy 6:6 KJV)

Printed in the United States
By Bookmasters